WOMEN IN
PHYSICAL SCIENCE

by Jodie Mangor

Content Consultant
Deborah Coen
Professor of History
Barnard College, Columbia University

Core Library

An Imprint of Abdo Publishing
abdopublishing.com

abdopublishing.com

Published by Abdo Publishing, a division of ABDO, PO Box 398166, Minneapolis, Minnesota 55439. Copyright © 2017 by Abdo Consulting Group, Inc. International copyrights reserved in all countries. No part of this book may be reproduced in any form without written permission from the publisher. Core Library™ is a trademark and logo of Abdo Publishing.

Printed in the United States of America, North Mankato, Minnesota
032016
092016

Cover Photo: Colin Cuthbert/Science Source
Interior Photos: Colin Cuthbert/Science Source, 1; Andrew Brookes/National Physical Laboratory/Science Source, 4; Robbie Shone/Science Source, 8, 43; iStockphoto, 10; SPL/Science Source, 12; Science Source, 16, 21, 45; Tony Freeman/Science Source, 18; Mark Garlick/Science Source, 24; Glenn Asakawa/The Denver Post/Getty Images, 26; Red Line Editorial, 28; Pontus Lundahl/AFP/Getty Images, 31; RIA Novosti/Science Source, 34; Joe Tucciarone/Science Source, 38; NASA, 40

Editor: Arnold Ringstad
Series Designer: Laura Polzin

Cataloging-in-Publication Data
Names: Mangor, Jodie, author.
Title: Women in physical science / by Jodie Mangor.
Description: Minneapolis, MN : Abdo Publishing, [2017] | Series: Women in
    STEM | Includes bibliographical references and index.
Identifiers: LCCN 2015960519 | ISBN 9781680782691 (lib. bdg.) |
    ISBN 9781680776805 (ebook)
Subjects: LCSH: Physical science--Juvenile literature.
Classification: DDC 500--dc23
LC record available at http://lccn.loc.gov/2015960519

CONTENTS

CHAPTER ONE

WOMEN SCIENTISTS: ONWARD AND UPWARD!

The universe is a fascinating place. Throughout history, men and women have wanted to know more about it. They developed the field of physical science. This branch of science explores all nonliving things.

Over and over, women have shown they can do great things in science when given the opportunity. They have made amazing discoveries. Their findings

Women around the world are using advanced technology to make new discoveries in physical science.

reach from the tiniest particles to distant stars. They have changed how we view the world.

What Is Physical Science?

The term *physical science* is broad. It covers the study of all nonliving matter and energy. It includes fields such as astronomy, physics, chemistry, and Earth science. Astronomy is the study of outer space. Physics looks at how energy and matter interact. Chemistry is the study of how matter changes. Earth science focuses on our planet. It includes everything from the planet's core to its atmosphere. Each field of physical science can be divided into many subfields.

Where Are the Women?

More than half of all US college students are women. Unfortunately, the percentage of women studying physical science is far below this. In 2014 women earned only 20 percent of all US bachelor's degrees in physics. In that same year, only 18 percent of working physicists and astronomers were women. So why aren't there more women in physical science?

Women have not had the same rights and opportunities as men. Social biases have held them back. They have had to struggle to get education. They have had to push to get science jobs. And often they have not gotten credit for their discoveries.

Many women scientists have faced some or all of these obstacles. But they have not let this stop them. These women work for the love of science.

IN THE REAL WORLD
The Nobel Prize

The Nobel Prize is one of the highest honors in the world. People who do outstanding work in specific fields can win it. It is given out in six areas: physics, chemistry, medicine, literature, peace, and economics. Different institutions decide who will get each award. The winner of a Nobel Prize is called a Nobel Laureate.

Nobel Prizes were first given out in 1901. Between 1901 and 2015, only five women won Nobel Prizes in physics or chemistry. Marie Curie won in both physics and chemistry. Maria Goeppert Mayer also received a Nobel Prize in physics. Irène Joliot-Curie, Dorothy Crowfoot Hodgkin, and Ada Yonath received prizes in chemistry.

Physical science research draws explorers to caves deep underground.

The Proof Is in the Science

Women have had to work hard to prove themselves in physical science fields. The road has been a hard one. Luckily, that is changing. We live in exciting times. Many people realize how important it is to have more women in science. Having diverse researchers and perspectives makes science stronger. More girls are being encouraged to study science. They are better supported in college. Women scientists have more opportunities.

Every day, many women around the world study physical science. They follow their interests to the bottom of the ocean, to the edges of outer space, or into the center of an atom. They notice new details and solve problems. They discover why things happen the way they do. And they inspire others.

No one knows what these explorers will find next. But it is certain that their curiosity will lead them to exciting new discoveries. Their work is important. It teaches us more about our world.

CHAPTER TWO

SMALL IN SIZE BUT NOT IN IMPORTANCE

Atoms are essential to our world. These basic units make up all the matter around us. Both physicists and chemists study atoms. Physicists study their structure. Chemists study their properties. They learn how atoms interact with each other. Women have made important discoveries about atoms and the even smaller particles within them.

Illustrations of atoms commonly show a nucleus surrounded by orbiting electrons.

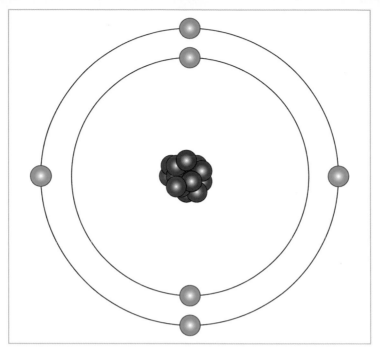

Nuclear Model

An atom's protons and neutrons are located in its center. They are surrounded by the atom's electrons. This diagram shows a carbon atom. Protons are shown in red, and neutrons are shown in blue. Electrons are shown in green. This diagram is not to scale. In reality, the nucleus is 10,000 times smaller than the entire atom. The electrons are as much as 500,000 times smaller than the nucleus. Why do you think it might be useful to think about atoms using a diagram that is not to scale?

A New Nuclear Model

What does the center, or nucleus, of an atom look like? Maria Goeppert Mayer came up with the nuclear shell model in the 1940s. It explains how particles called protons and neutrons are arranged in the nucleus. It also explains why some atoms are more stable than others. Stable atoms can hold their protons and neutrons in place permanently. Unstable atoms may shed some of these particles.

Another scientist, J. Hans D. Jensen, studied atoms at the same time as Goeppert Mayer. They worked separately, but they came to the same conclusions. Together they wrote a book about the nuclear shell model. Their work changed the way scientists understood atoms. They were both awarded the Nobel Prize in Physics in 1963.

Hunting for Heavy Elements

Darleane Hoffman also studies atoms. She has had a long career as a scientific hunter. She hunts for heavy elements.

An element is a substance made from only one type of atom. Each element has its own atomic number. This number is equal to the number of protons in each atom's nucleus. Heavy elements have atomic numbers greater than 92.

In 1971 Hoffman found the first example of element 94 in nature. It is also called plutonium. Before, plutonium could only be created in laboratories. Hoffman found plutonium in rock that was several billion years old.

It is difficult to make heavy elements in the lab. Scientists use a machine to shoot one element at a target made of another element. The elements combine to make a new heavy element. They are all radioactive.

Hoffman was part of a lab team that confirmed the existence of element

106 in 1994. She also made two new forms of element 110, and she did studies on elements 105 and 103.

Hoffman is a recognized expert on heavy elements. She has trained a new generation of element hunters. Teams in Germany, Russia, and the United States are now making heavy elements with atomic numbers above 110.

In 2000 the American Chemical Society presented Hoffman with the Priestley Medal. This is its highest honor.

The Stuff That Things Are Made Of

Elementary particles are the very smallest building blocks of matter. They make up all things. They cannot be divided into anything smaller. For many years, scientists thought the atom was an elementary particle. Then they discovered atoms are made of even smaller particles. These are called protons, neutrons, and electrons. The electron is an elementary particle. Protons and neutrons are made of quarks. Other elementary particles include the gluon, muon, tau, photon, and Higgs boson. Elementary particles are also called subatomic particles.

Atom smashers are often built in enormous loops.

Smashing Atoms!

Instead of creating atoms, Melissa Franklin smashes them. She helps build and operate atom smashers. These machines are also called particle accelerators. They are big and complicated. They can make atoms travel at incredible speeds.

When atoms smash together, they break apart. Scientists can detect the even smaller particles within them. Franklin searches for these amazingly tiny objects. She studies what they are and how they interact.

To find the answers, Franklin worked with thousands of other physicists from many different countries. Her team discovered two particles. They are called the top quark and the Higgs boson.

FURTHER EVIDENCE

Chapter Two included information about element hunter Darleane Hoffman. What was one of the main points of this section? What evidence supported this point? The website below includes more details about Hoffman's life and work. Does the information on the website support one of the points in Chapter Two? Does it present new evidence?

Chemical Heritage Foundation: Darleane Hoffman

mycorelibrary.com/women-in-physical-science

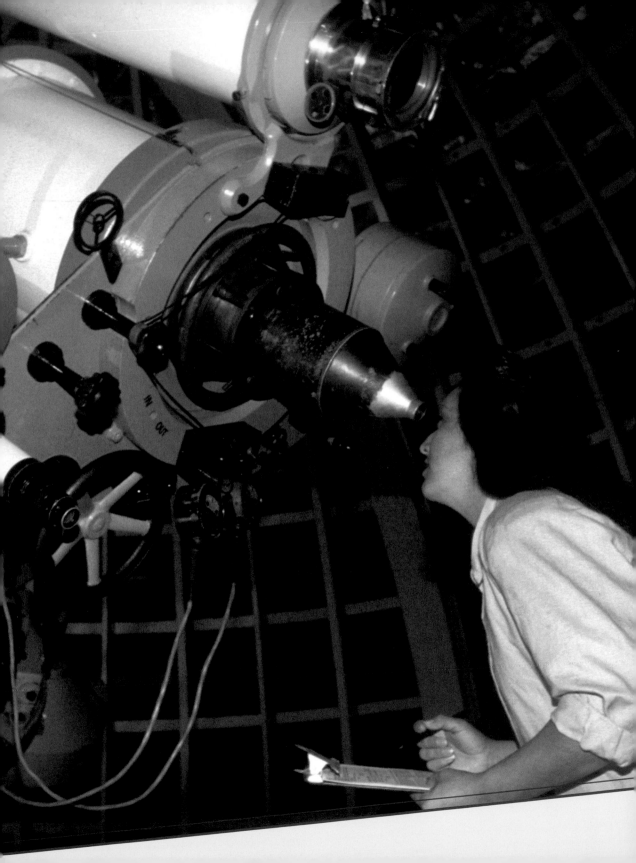

CHAPTER THREE

ASTRONOMICAL DISCOVERIES

For thousands of years, women have studied the night sky. Some are curious about stars. Others search for new planets. They ask questions about space. Where did the universe come from? How did the universe form? Is there life on other planets? These insightful astronomers help us understand how our universe works.

Astronomers use huge telescopes to peer into the night sky.

Dark Matter Matters

Scientists sometimes come across results they don't expect. This happened to Vera Rubin in the 1970s. What she discovered would change the way we view the universe.

Rubin was measuring how fast stars orbit in spiral galaxies. She expected stars near the edges to move slower than those near the center. She expected this based on what she knew about gravity.

Gravity is an important force in space. It affects the way objects move. There is gravitational pull between objects. The closer

What Are Stars Made Of?

In the early 1900s, Cecilia Payne-Gaposchkin wondered what stars are made of. She studied the spectra, or light patterns, of stars. Her research showed that all stars have a similar chemical makeup. She found that they mainly contain hydrogen and helium. These are the two lightest elements in the universe. Her work was an important step in understanding what makes up the universe.

Scientists have colored the suspected location of dark matter blue in this image.

two objects are to each other, the more pull there is. The more pull, the faster the objects can move while remaining in orbit. The edges of galaxies have less visible matter than their centers. So scientists expected the pull of gravity to be weaker there. That would make the orbits slower.

Instead Rubin found that stars near the edge orbit just as fast as stars near the center. The discovery means there must be more matter we cannot see. Scientists called this invisible matter *dark matter*.

Rubin calculated that there must be a large amount of it in the universe.

New Planet Detector

Dark matter remains mysterious, but there is still much to discover about the visible universe. For example, are there other planets like Earth? Do we share the universe with other living beings? Natalie Batalha explores the frontiers of space. She hopes to answer these questions. She's part of a team that hunts for exoplanets. These planets lie outside our solar system. They orbit around stars other than our sun.

Batalha uses the *Kepler* spacecraft, which carries a telescope designed for exoplanet research. She has been part of the *Kepler* mission from its start. NASA launched the spacecraft in 2009. By 2015 it had helped find more than 1,000 planets. A handful of these are small, rocky, and Earth-like.

Kepler finds planets by watching stars. Sometimes a star's brightness dips, then goes back to normal. This may mean one of that star's planets crossed in front of it. *Kepler* watches for these dips to find evidence of exoplanets.

The Biggest Bursts of Them All!

Gamma-ray bursts (GRB) are some of the most dramatic events in the universe. These bursts of light are about a million trillion times brighter than our sun. They happen approximately once a day.

Chryssa Kouveliotou started studying GRBs when they were still a complete mystery. She helped prove they come from outside our galaxy. She also discovered there are two different kinds of GRBs. Some last less than a second. Others last minutes.

IN THE REAL WORLD

Satellites in Science

A satellite is an object that orbits around a larger object. People build and launch satellites into space. Some are used to send TV and phone signals around the world. Others are used as tools for scientific research. They carry cameras and scientific sensors. As they orbit Earth or other bodies, they take photos and collect data.

A GRB happens when a black hole forms. A black hole is an area in space with a very strong gravitational pull and is believed to be created by the collapse of a massive star. The energy of the collapse releases extremely powerful gamma rays.

In 1996 Vera Rubin spoke to the graduating class at the University of California, Berkeley:

> *Individually, you will be called by many names: spouse, partner, teacher, professor, writer, representative, president, CEO, doctor, judge, regent. Some will be called scientists. For those of you who teach science, I hope that you will welcome, as students, those who do NOT intend to be scientists, as well as those who DO. We need senators who have studied physics and representatives who understand ecology.*
>
> *And for those of you who choose to be scientists, I have one piece of advice. Don't give up. Science is hard and demanding, but each of you must believe that you can succeed. It may seem unlikely tonight, but there is not one among you who cannot make important, major contributions to the world of science.*

Source: Vera Rubin. Bright Galaxies, Dark Matters. *Woodbury, NY: American Institute of Physics, 1997. Print. 218.*

Consider Your Audience

Review this passage closely. Write a blog post conveying this same information for a new audience. What is the most effective way to get your point across to this audience? How does your post differ from the original text and why?

CHAPTER FOUR

LASERS, LIGHT, AND CRYSTALS

Many women scientists are pioneers. They create new tools to expand the frontiers of science. Some of their discoveries are useful in other fields too. They may help biologists or engineers.

Ultrafast Lasers

Margaret Murnane builds ultrafast lasers. They flash on and off to make the fastest strobe lights in the

Murnane, *left*, works on a laser alongside her students at the University of Colorado.

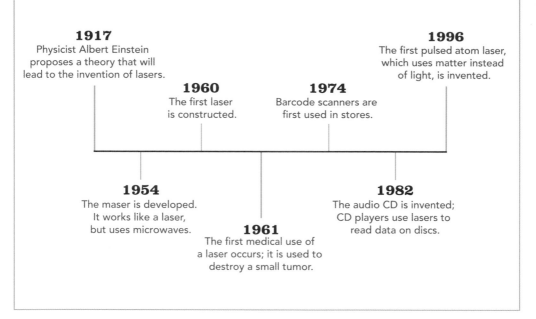

1917
Physicist Albert Einstein proposes a theory that will lead to the invention of lasers.

1960
The first laser is constructed.

1974
Barcode scanners are first used in stores.

1996
The first pulsed atom laser, which uses matter instead of light, is invented.

1954
The maser is developed. It works like a laser, but uses microwaves.

1961
The first medical use of a laser occurs; it is used to destroy a small tumor.

1982
The audio CD is invented; CD players use lasers to read data on discs.

Laser Milestones

The first laser was built in 1960. Since then, scientists keep finding more ways to use lasers. They have become a regular part of our day-to-day lives. Which examples of lasers on this timeline have you encountered in your daily life?

world. Each flash lasts for less than a femtosecond. That's one quadrillionth of a second. These lasers act like camera flashes. They can be used to record electrons buzzing around atoms.

Thousands of lasers have now been built using Murnane's technology. They are used all over the world for research in physics, chemistry, biology, and engineering.

Slowing Down Light

Light is the fastest thing in the universe. It moves at a constant speed of approximately 186,282 miles per second (300,000 km/s). At the speed of light, you could circle Earth seven times in just one second. Imagine slowing light from this speed down to a stop.

Lene Vestergaard Hau has found a way to do it. First she cools atoms of the element sodium to extremely cold temperatures. They become a cloud of gas. Then she shines a beam of light at the cloud. Inside the cold gas, the light slows down and stops moving. It also shortens. The beam changes from 0.6 miles (1 km) in length to only .0008 inches (0.02 mm).

IN THE REAL WORLD

Lighting up the Future

Physicists and other scientists have invented many ways to use light. Lasers are used in DVD players. They are also used for surgery. Light signals sent through tiny optical fibers transmit information across the Internet.

Under these conditions, Hau can move the light around. She can also make it speed up again. Controlling light is an exciting new area of science to explore.

X-Ray Crystallography

When a material crystallizes, its molecules organize into repeating patterns. If a beam of X-rays is directed at the crystal, some of the X-rays will pass through it. Others will bounce off in a specific pattern. The pattern shows how atoms are arranged. It can be used to figure out a molecule's structure. Crystallography has helped scientists make many important discoveries.

Impossible Crystals

Another frontier-expanding area is crystallography. This branch of science uses chemistry and physics to figure out the structure of molecules. It helps answer many questions.

For years, scientists around the world tried to understand how ribosomes work. Ribosomes create proteins. These are one

Yonath, *left*, accepts the Nobel Prize from King Carl XVI
Gustaf of Sweden.

of the basic building blocks of life. They are found in every living cell.

Ada Yonath decided to approach the problem with crystallography. She wanted to determine what a ribosome looked like. This could help explain how it works.

First Yonath needed crystals of ribosomes. It would be very difficult to make them. Ribosomes flop around and are unstable. They contain approximately a million individual atoms. Other scientists did not believe she could do it.

Yonath developed a way to do crystallography at freezing temperatures. It worked! She was able to make ribosome crystals and analyze them. In 2001 she published the complete structure of a ribosome. Eight years later, she won the Nobel Prize in Chemistry for her work.

In 2009 Ada Yonath was awarded the Nobel Prize. In her acceptance speech, she noted how other scientists first viewed her ideas:

> Indeed, words originating from the verb "to die" were frequently used when I described my initial plans to determine the ribosome structure. Many distinguished scientists said: 'why work on ribosomes, they are dead. . . we know all what can be known about them', or: 'this is a dead end road', or: 'you will be dead before you get there'. To my satisfaction, these predictions were proven wrong, the ribosomes are alive and kicking (so am I) and their high resolution structures stimulated more advanced studies as well as the imagination of many youngsters, including my granddaughter, Noa, who is showing continuous interest, and invited me at the ages of 5 and 13 to explain to her classes what the ribosome is.
>
> Source: Ada Yonath. "Banquet Speech." NobelPrize.org. Nobel Media, 2009. Web. Accessed February 8, 2016.

Point of View

At the end of Chapter Three, there is a quote from a speech by Vera Rubin. Read it and compare Rubin's and Yonath's points of view. Write a short essay that answers the following questions: What is the point of view of each speaker? How are they similar and why? How are they different and why?

CHAPTER FIVE

GETTING DOWN TO EARTH

The world is full of mysteries. Women in the field of Earth science are helping solve them. They study the air, land, and water. They examine how these things interact with each other and impact life on the planet. Their work is guided by the questions they want to answer. What does the bottom of the ocean look like? What events caused dinosaurs to go

Specialized vehicles take scientists to hard-to-reach places, such as the bottom of the sea.

extinct? And why do volcanoes behave the way they do?

Modern-Day Explorer

Julia Morgan studies how rock structures change. As part of her work, she explores places that have never been seen before. Morgan goes on research cruises. On the ships, she uses sound waves to study layers of rocks at the bottom of the ocean.

Morgan has also traveled miles below the ocean's surface. She explored the deepest parts of the ocean floor near Hawaii. A deep-sea research vessel called the *Shinkai 6500* carried her down. It allowed

Mapping the Ocean Floor with Sound Waves

It is not always possible to see to the bottom of the ocean. Scientists use a technology called sonar to learn about these great depths. Sonar uses sound waves and their echoes. Scientists study how sound waves bounce off the sea floor and return to the surface as echoes. They use this information to create a detailed map of the ocean floor.

Morgan to collect rocks from an underwater landslide. Morgan's studies help us understand geological events of the past and present.

Major Impact

The Earth's surface holds clues about its past history. One longstanding mystery is why the dinosaurs went extinct 65 million years ago. What wiped them out? Adriana C. Ocampo Uria may have found the answer. She helped discover a giant crater on Mexico's Yucatán peninsula. The Chicxulub crater is 125 miles (200 km) wide. An asteroid or comet struck Earth and formed it. The impact may have caused a mass extinction.

Ocampo Uria first saw evidence of the crater on satellite images. Geologists use photos like this to study Earth's surface. Scientists also use cameras in space to study other planets, moons, comets, and asteroids.

Scientists believe the asteroid or comet that created the Chicxulub crater was approximately 6 miles (10 km) wide.

Volcanoes in Space

Rosaly Lopes-Gautier studies volcanoes in space. She learns about the physics behind volcanic eruptions. In space, magma is made up of different materials than on Earth. Volcanoes on other planets or moons exist within different atmospheres. They are affected by more or less gravity than the volcanoes on Earth. Volcanoes on other planets can be much bigger than on Earth. Studying volcanoes under different conditions will help scientists better understand them on Earth.

IN THE REAL WORLD

Becoming Scientists

Careers in science, technology, engineering, and math (STEM) often have good salaries. But many smart, creative women who might have been great scientists choose other jobs. Schools and companies are taking steps to change that. They are showing girls how exciting science can be. They are training teachers and staff to give women more support. And experienced women scientists are acting as role models and mentors.

Jupiter's moon Io is covered in more than 400 volcanoes.

In 2006 Lopes-Gautier was honored in the
Guinness Book of World Records. She had discovered
the most active volcanoes anywhere. She found 71
on Jupiter's moon Io. She has also visited dozens of

volcanoes on Earth. Lopes-Gautier has written several books. One is called *The Volcano Adventure Guide*. It contains information about how to explore volcanoes safely.

This is an exciting time for girls and women to get involved in physical science. Opportunities for women are improving. Women are being encouraged to study science. Female physical scientists keep making great discoveries. They inspire us. The work of women in physical science will continue to push the boundaries of our knowledge in the future.

EXPLORE ONLINE

Chapter Five discusses volcanoes in space. The website below tells how volcanoes were discovered on Jupiter's moon Io. How does the information from the website expand on what was presented in Chapter Five? What new information did you learn from the website?

Space Volcano Explorer

mycorelibrary.com/women-in-physical-science

Unlock the Secrets of the Universe

Interested in the universe and how it works? You can start exploring space by going outside on a clear night. Observe the stars. Use a pair of binoculars or a telescope. Note what you see. Write down any questions. Then read astronomy books and websites about the night sky. Try to find the answers to the questions you wrote down.

Earth Science in Your Neighborhood

Physical scientists are curious about the world around them. Observe whether the area you live in is hilly or flat. Is there a lot of rock, sand, or clay? Where is the nearest body of water? Draw a map and label it with your observations. Read books about Earth science. Ask a teacher or librarian to help you do research online to find out what made the land the way it is.

Element Hunting

Print out a copy of the periodic table, which lists all of the elements. Then go on an element hunt, alone or with friends. Using books and websites as resources, figure out what elements are in the objects around you. Then highlight those elements on the periodic table. See how many you can find.

Tell the Tale

Chapter Three of this book discusses new discoveries in space. Imagine you are an astronomer who has just discovered a new exoplanet that appears to have life on it. Write 200 words about your observations, what they mean, and what your next steps will be to study these new forms of life.

Another View

This book focuses on the research and discoveries of female physical scientists. Find another source about women in science and their work. Write a short essay comparing and contrasting the point of view of this new source with that of this book's author. What is the point of view of each author? How are they similar and why? How are they different and why?

Surprise Me

Chapter Four discusses new innovations related to light and lasers. After reading this book, what two or three facts about this area of study did you find most surprising? Write a few sentences about each fact.

Dig Deeper

After reading this book, what questions do you still have about physical science and the universe around you? With an adult's help, find a few reliable sources that can help you answer your questions. Write a paragraph about what you learned.

GLOSSARY

asteroid
a small rocky object that travels around the sun

bias
an unfair prejudice against a particular person or group of people

femtosecond
1/1,000,000,000,000,000 of a second

galaxy
a very large group of stars

geological
having to do with Earth's physical structure

magma
hot liquid rock found beneath a planet's surface

matter
the substances that make up the physical world

molecule
the smallest possible amount of a substance that still contains all of its characteristics

nuclear
relating to the nucleus of atoms

orbit
to travel around something in a curved path

radioactive
made up of atoms that give off harmful radiation as their nuclei break down

structure
how something is arranged or put together

LEARN MORE

Books

Rowell, Rebecca. *Marie Curie Advances the Study of Radioactivity*. Minneapolis, MN: Abdo Publishing, 2016.

Yasuda, Anita. *Astronomy: Cool Women in Space*. White River Junction, VT: Nomad Press, 2015.

Websites

To learn more about Women in STEM, visit **booklinks.abdopublishing.com**. These links are routinely monitored and updated to provide the most current information available.

Visit **mycorelibrary.com** for free additional tools for teachers and students.

INDEX

ABOUT THE AUTHOR

Jodie Mangor puts her degrees in biology and environmental science to work by editing scientific papers. Her stories, poems, and articles have appeared in a variety of children's magazines. She lives in Ithaca, New York, with her family.